Fire Safety for Kids

Published by Gateway Community Safety Net
TOLL-FREE TELEPHONE: 1.800.665.4878

Gateway Publishing Co., Ltd.   AND   **Gateway Publishing Co., Inc.**
385 DeBaets Street   276 Cavalier Street, P.O. Box 559
Winnipeg, MB R2J 4J8   Pembina, ND 58271-0559

www.communitysafetynet.com

ISBN 0-920030-31-9
Printed and bound in Canada

This book is recommended for young people aged 7 to 11.

Researched and compiled by
KATHLEEN FRASER

Updated by
KEVIN ROSEN

PARK FALLS
VOLUNTEER FIRE DEPARTMENT
PARK FALLS, WI

as a

COMMUNITY SAFETY ADVOCATE

for outstanding commitment to child safety

Partners In Safety

Protecting kids for LIFE

The following partners are proud supporters of the local

Community Safety Net initiative. We're privileged to

have these community Partners in Safety helping to

educate and protect our most precious resource.

CLASS PARTNER

FLAMBEAU HOSPITAL
98 Sherry Avenue, Park Falls, WI 54552
(715) 762-2484

1/2 CLASS PARTNER

PARK FALLS FIRE/RESCUE DEPARTMENT
Park Falls, WI

Partners In Safety

Protecting kids for **LIFE**

1/3 CLASS PARTNERS

BOB'S FACTORY OUTLET – 3 FLOORS OF FURNITURE
(715) 762-2855

CHR HOME HEALTH CARE
(715) 762-4600

FIRST NATIONAL BANK OF PARK FALLS
(715) 762-2411

GUSTAFSON'S IGA
(715) 762-4272

H & R BLOCK
(715) 762-3636

NORTHERN MERCHANDISE
(715) 762-4464

PAMIDA
(715) 762-2959

PARK MANOR NURSING HOME
(715) 762-2449

T'S AUTOMOTIVE
(715) 762-2044

WOLLERMAN, INC.
(715) 762-4626

Partners In Safety
Protecting kids for LIFE

SUPPORTING PARTNERS

NAPA AUTO PARTS

NEW YORK LIFE - JAMES KRONBERGER

SCHRAUFNAGEL'S AUTO GLASS

SOUTH SIDE TRUE VALUE

STATE FARM INSURANCE – DIANA L. HERBST

SUPER ONE FOODS

HEGSTROM JEWELERS

NORTHERN ENVIRONMENTAL

THE GIFT CORNER

ANONYMOUS

ART'S BARBER & STYLING

UPPER STREET APPAREL

D & D TIRE & AUTO CENTER, INC.

HOLIDAY OF PARK FALLS, INC.

NOTE TO PARENTS: This book is intended to help kids live safely. Its aim is to teach that, by understanding and observing a collection of simple rules, young people can stay happy, healthy, and SAFE.

Other safety programs available from Gateway Safety Net Publications:

	SUGGESTED AGES
• Personal Safety for Kids	9 – 12
• Farm Safety for Kids	9 and up
• Drug Safety: The Choice is Yours	10 and up
• Safety First Nations	10 and up

this book belongs to:

My first name is: _____

My last name is: _____

My telephone number is: _____

My address is: _____

I live in the city/town of: _____

I attend school at:

_____

My birthday is on:

_____

This book is dedicated to all firefighters and other emergency service providers, including those who lost their lives in the rescue efforts surrounding the tragic events of September 11th, 2001.

table of contents

ACKNOWLEDGEMENTS   8

GLOSSARY OF TERMS: 9

A FIREFIGHTER'S POEM   10

PART ONE: INTRODUCTION
1.1 Fire Statistics   12
1.2 Fire Has Many Good Uses   14
1.3 Fire Can Harm, Too   16
1.4 Fire Departments   18

PART TWO: PREVENTING FIRES
2.1 How Do Fires Start?   22
2.2 Fire Safety In The Home   24
2.3 Holiday Hazards   27
2.4 Other Things That Can Burn   30
2.5 Symbols To Avoid   36
2.6 No Smoking, Please   38
2.7 Review The Rules   39

PART THREE: BEING PREPARED
3.1 Smoke Alarms   44
3.2 Escape Plans   46
3.3 My Escape Plan   49
3.4 Fire Drills   50

PART FOUR: RESPONDING TO EMERGENCIES
4.1 When You Hear The Siren   54
4.2 If You See A Fire In Your Home   55
4.3 If You See A Fire Away From Home   59
4.4 Calling 9-1-1   60
4.5 Pet Safety During A Fire   61

PART FIVE: OUTDOOR FIRE SAFETY
5.1 Forest Fires   64
5.2 Campfires   65
5.3 Other Outdoor Fire Safety Rules   67

PART SIX: FIRE SAFETY FOR CAREGIVERS
6.1 Encourage Learning   70
6.2 Rules For Parents   71
6.3 Rules For Teachers   78
6.4 Rules For Babysitters   79
6.5 More Information   80

PART SEVEN: FIRST AID TIPS
7.1 Hypothermia   82
7.2 Burns And Scalds   83
7.3 Unconsciousness   83
7.4 Fractures   84
7.5 Heat Exhaustion   85
7.6 Frostbite   85
7.7 Eye Injuries   86
7.8 Medication   87
7.9 Nose Bleeds   87
7.10 Embedded Object   88
7.11 Snake Bite   88
7.12 Wounds and Bleeding   89
7.13 Artificial Respiration   90
7.14 Conscious Choking Casualty   91
7.15 Unconscious Choking Casualty   92

PART EIGHT: FUN, LEARNING & GRADUATION
8.1 Fill In The Blanks   94
8.2 Fire Safety Quiz   95
8.3 Coloring Time!   100
8.4 Games & Puzzles   107
8.5 Autographs   112
8.6 Important Telephone Numbers   113
8.7 Diploma   114
8.8 Safety Pledge   115
8.9 Mr. Computer Contest   116

acknowledgements

I n researching this book, we appreciate the contributions (both direct and indirect) of the following organizations and institutions:

- Alliant Energy (powerhousetv.com)
- American Humane Society (americanhumane.org)
- Consumer and Corporate Affairs Canada
- Federal Bureau of Investigation
- Fire Commissioners of Manitoba
- Fire Prevention Branch of the City of Winnipeg Fire Dept.
- Health and Welfare Canada
- Hermon Fire Department
- Manitoba Health
- National Fire Protection Association (NFPA)
- SEMCO Energy
- SOS KIDS Babysitting Agency
- St. John Ambulance
- The American Human Association
- US Department of Justice
- Winnipeg Public Library

We applaud the willingness of so many diverse organizations to help today's youth live happy and successful lives.

glossary of terms

To help explain the rules of fire safety, this book uses some words that you may not already know. This glossary explains some of these terms. If you come across a word that you don't understand, check here to see if it's listed. If not, look in a dictionary or ask an adult to help you find out the word's meaning.

COMBUSTIBLE: something that can easily catch fire or burn

CORROSIVE: a chemical that gradually wears away or destroys what it touches

FLAMMABLE: see "combustible"

FLASHOVER: when all items in a room become super-heated and burst into flames at the same time

IGNITE: to start on fire or begin to burn

PILOT LIGHT: a small fire that heats the air or water in a furnace or hot water tank

SCALD: to be burned by hot liquid or steam

a firefighter's poem

When I am called to duty,
Wherever flames may rage;
It is my goal to save some life,
Whatever be its age.
I hope to embrace a little child
Before it is too late;
Or save an older person from
The horror of that fate.
I strive to be alert
And hear the weakest shout,
And quickly and efficiently,
To put the fire out.
In the face of danger
I will give the best in me;
To guard my every neighbor and
Protect his/her property.
And if in the line of duty
I have to lose my life,
I know my bravery will make proud
My children and my husband/wife

part

introduction

one

fire statistics

- In the United States and Canada, a home fire is reported to fire departments every 80 seconds.

- Every two and a half hours, someone in the U.S. or Canada dies in a home fire.

- Fire causes $5.5 billion worth of property damage annually in the U.S and $2.1 billion annually in Canada.

- The civilian fire death rate in the U.S. is 14.8 deaths per million people; it is 13.5 deaths per million people in Canada.

- Home fire is the disaster that children are most likely to experience.

- Home fire is the fifth leading cause of unintentional injury in the U.S.

- Fire is the leading cause of death for children under the age of 15 at home.

- 40% of fires that kill young children are started by children playing with fire.

- Smoking materials account for roughly 25% of civilian home fire deaths.

- About 80% of all fire deaths occur where people sleep (such as homes, dormitories, and hotels).

- Roughly 80% of home fire deaths occur where a smoke alarm is not present or operating.

- Most fatal fires occur when people are less likely to be alert, such as nighttime sleeping hours.

- **Nearly all home and other building fires are preventable.**

Statistics from the National Fire Protection Association (NFPA)

fire has many good uses

Fire was discovered a long, long time ago. Since then, people have learned how to use it for many things. For one, they found that most food tasted better after it had been cooked. In the early days, this was done outdoors, over an open fire (like the campfires we might see today).

When homes became more modern, people began to cook indoors. They would heat the food in pots, which they'd hang above burning wood or coal. Sometimes, they'd use a "spit" to cook meat. A "spit" is a long rod placed above a fire. It can be turned to keep meat from burning and to cook it evenly.

When stoves were invented, cooking became easier. Today, we have stoves that use coal, oil, gas, and electricity. Many of us have microwave ovens in our homes, too.

Even though we do most of our cooking in the home, sometimes we cook outdoors, too. Barbecues are used to grill food and give it a tasty flavor. Campfires can be used

to cook at picnics and cookouts.

MORE THAN COOKING
But fire and heat are used to help us do lots of other important things besides cooking. For example, it helps us to wash. Most homes have a water heater, which heats cold water for us to use. That way we can enjoy a warm bath, wash our dishes in hot water, and do some of our laundry in warm or hot water.

If you live where it gets cold in winter, your home may have a fireplace to help you keep warm. Your house may also have a furnace, which moves heated air around to all the rooms.

So as you can see, fire (and heat) play an important role in our lives. It keeps us comfortable and makes life easier in many ways.

fire can harm, too

E ven though we use fire to help us cook, wash, and stay warm, there are some fires that we really don't want. Those are ones that start on their own or happen where they shouldn't. You see, fire can destroy our homes and our belongings. It can also hurt us very badly.

That's why it's so important to be VERY careful when it comes to fire.

Fortunately, there are rules we can follow to help ensure that fire doesn't hurt us or our friends, family, pets, and other people. The rules aren't hard to learn or remember, if we try. So here's the good news: *if we're smart about fire safety, then we don't have to be afraid*.

This book will help us learn what to do (and what not to do) when it comes to fire. So be sure to read it all the way through and share it with your family members and

friends (show your parents *Part Six: Fire Safety For Caregivers* on Page 69).

Should you come across any words you don't understand, try checking

> **FIRE SAFETY TIP**
> Never play with or near anything that makes fire.

the glossary on page 9. If that doesn't help, ask your teacher, a parent, or an adult you know to explain it to you. When you're finished with the book, put it somewhere safe. You can come back to it whenever you need to refresh your memory on the rules of fire safety.

fire departments

Before fire engines were invented, most fires were fought by small groups of people who would throw water on the flames. The first fire engines were much smaller than those we see today and were pulled by men or horses. Eventually, fire hoses, ladders, and fire hydrants made firefighting easier.

Today, we have very good firefighting equipment. It allows firefighters to reach high buildings and into other places that they couldn't go before. That means most fires can be put out quickly if  the fire department is alerted soon enough. It's possible to save more lives, homes, and buildings.

BIG OR SMALL

The size of a community's fire department depends on how many people there are to protect. Big cities and towns have more than one fire station or fire hall. They have many firetrucks (fire engines) and lots of firefighters. In smaller towns, there is often only one firetruck and just the number of firefighters needed to work with it.

Some small communities don't have their own fire department. They have to call on the one from a nearby town or city when help is needed.

In some places, there is a volunteer fire department. That means the firefighters have other jobs when they're not putting out fires, since the community is not large enough to need full-time firefighters.

REAL LIFE HEROES
No matter what kind of fire department you have where you live, the firefighters are always ready to rush to a fire. You can be sure they'll get there as soon as possible and do their best to put it out quickly. That's because firefighters are very brave, dedicated people. They're committed to protecting their communities and saving lives — even if it means putting their own lives in danger.

OTHER ACTIVITIES
When they're not fighting fires, firefighters do many other things for their communities. Some collect money for

children and adults who have been burned in fires. The funds are used to help pay for their care in hospital or at home.

Some firefighters repair toys and give them to needy children at Christmas. Many fire departments also send firefighters out to schools, so they can teach children about fire safety. They also go to nursing homes and hospitals to make sure the residents and patients know what to do if a fire breaks out.

FIRE SAFETY TIP
If you hear a fire engine coming, be sure to stay clear of the street.

part
preventing
fires
two

how do fires start?

Many things that are very hot can start a fire. It happens when something hot is too close to something that will burn. Think about what happens when food gets too much heat. It burns, right? Well, the same thing can happen to other items if they get too hot, and some will actually catch on fire.

That's why the kitchen is a dangerous place for kids to play. If you get too close to a hot stove, your toys could get damaged. Your clothes could catch on fire. Or you could get badly burned. So it's very important that you **remember not to play in the kitchen**, especially when someone is using the oven.

DON'T PLAY AROUND
Never play with matches or lighters. These items can start fires, so it's important to remember that they're NOT toys. If you find a book of

matches or a lighter, give it to an adult and ask him or her to put it somewhere safe.

FLASHOVER

Flashover happens when all items in a room, from an armchair to the TV set, become super-heated and burst into flames at the same time. Flashover can happen in as little as three minutes after the fire starts.

Fire is fast. In 30 seconds, a simple flame can get completely out of control. That's how quickly curtains catching fire from a space heater can turn into a major fire. In as little as two minutes, the room can become life threatening. In as little as five minutes, your whole house can be on fire.

Fire is hot. The heat from a fire can be more dangerous than the flames. The air gets so hot, you can't breathe.

Fire is dark. You may think fire is bright, but inside a house it actually becomes very dark as smoke rolls down from the ceiling.

fire safety in the home

S adly, a lot of fires happen in homes where there are children. Many of these occur because someone didn't follow the rules of fire safety. So here are some important things to remember that will help you stay safe.

FIREPLACES

Do you have a fireplace inside your home? Many people do, because a fireplace can make a house very cozy on a

cold day. But if there is one in your house, you shouldn't get too close to it, or play near it (if you're unsure as to what's a safe distance, ask a parent). You should NEVER try to start a fire in the fireplace, and NEVER try to touch the fire or put something into it. That's because **you can be very badly burned if you get too close to a fire**. Leave it to your parents or a responsible adult to take care of the fireplace.

BARBECUES

Lots of people have a barbecue at home, too. That's because many of us enjoy having hotdogs, hamburgers, chicken, steaks, and other meals made on the barbecue. But the barbecue is not safe for children to touch or be near, because it gets really, REALLY hot. Even after it's been turned off, the barbecue will stay hot for quite a long

time. So you shouldn't go near it or touch it anytime. Remember, **only adults should use the barbecue,** and they must be sure to use it only when it's working properly.

FURNACES & HEATERS

Depending on when it was built, your house will have either "registers" or "radiators". Both of these warm up your home when it's cold by providing heat to various rooms. As a result, registers and radiators are very warm and sometimes very hot. That's why you shouldn't play close to them and never put anything that can burn on or within three feet of them. Otherwise, you could burn yourself or possibly cause a fire.

FIRE SAFETY TIP

Don't leave towels, clothes, or anything that can burn on a heater or radiator.

Another device used to warm homes is called a "portable heater". These heaters are light enough for an adult to carry, and they can be moved around to different rooms, as needed. Similar to a register or radiator, a portable heater can get very hot. That's why you should **NEVER touch or play with a portable heater.**

PILOT LIGHTS

If you have a furnace or a water heater in your home, there may be a "pilot light" under it. This is a very small fire that heats the air or water in the unit. But you must NEVER touch it. If you do, it will burn you!

WIRING & ELECTRICITY

Many things in your home — such as lights, the TV, and the fridge — require electricity to run. But if the wires (through which the electric current travels) get frayed or damaged, fires can start. That's why you must **NEVER touch or play with wires, plugs, or electrical outlets**. Ask your parents to watch for flickering lights or sparks when plugging in a device. If it happens, they should call an electrician.

holiday hazards

Duct the holiday season, many people put Christmas trees in their homes. Some trees are real and others are artificial (which means they are made of special materials and can be bought at a store). Both kinds are very beautiful, but we must be extremely careful when decorating them in our home.

Christmas tree lights get very hot and will burn you, if you touch them. If you play with the electric power cord, you could be badly burned or hurt by electricity. That's why, as

a rule, you should **never play with Christmas tree lights or their cords** (or touch electrical sockets). Your parents may let you help decorate the tree, but you must NEVER do it unless they are right there with you.

SPOOKY STUFF

Don't you just love Halloween? Kids love getting dressed up, and some adults do, too! But some costumes are made

out of materials that are **flammable** (that means easily set on fire). So before you get dressed up, have an adult **make sure that your costume is made of a non-flammable material**. The same goes for masks. Or better yet, just wear face paint. That way you'll be able to see better, and there will be no chance of your mask catching fire.

Another fun Halloween tradition is making and displaying a jack-o-lantern (a pumpkin with eyes and a mouth cut into it). Sometimes, jack-o-lanterns have lights inside of them to make them glow. If you're going to do this, always use a flashlight inside the pumpkin. **NEVER put a candle in the jack-o-lantern**. It's very dangerous, since it could start a fire.

MAKE A WISH

You probably enjoy birthday parties — especially when it's YOUR birthday party. That's because, in addition to receiving presents, you get to blow out the birthday candles. But the flame on candles is very hot and can burn. So

don't ever try to light the candles yourself (or touch them when they're lit). An adult should always be there to light the candles and supervise while you're blowing them out. That way you can enjoy your cake and not worry about anything except making a wish!

LOOK, BUT DON'T TOUCH

Fireworks can be lots of fun to watch. They make neat patterns and lots of noise. But they should only be handled by professionals who know how to use them. **Fireworks should never be set off by amateurs, and ESPECIALLY not children.** If they go off too soon or in the wrong place, they can cause burns, fire, and damage.

other things that can burn

U sually when we talk about burning, we think of fire and flames. But other things can burn us, too. For example, if we touch water that's too hot (like in the bathtub), we can be burned. This is called being "**scalded**", and it hurts a LOT. We can also be "scalded"

by the steam from a kettle, a sauna, a car's radiator — even from cooking food. A pot of very hot water on the stove can scald, and so can hot grease. That's another reason why you should never play in the kitchen.

TASTE TEST

Another way you can be burned is if you taste food that is too hot. It could burn your tongue, lips, and the roof of your mouth! **The best way to avoid burning yourself with food is to test a little bit first** and blow on it before putting it in your mouth.

SUMMER FUN

Do you like playing outside when the weather is warm? Being out in the sun is fun and relaxing, but can also be dangerous if you're not careful. On hot days, you might get sunburned on your skin, if you're not wearing sunscreen. Not only does a sunburn sting, it could cause health problems down the road. So **before you go out in the hot sun, ask a parent or an adult you trust to help you put sunscreen on** your skin. Then you can play in the sun without worries!

GASOLINE

Gasoline is a very useful chemical. It fuels engines, so cars can drive. But that's about all it should be used for. **Never**

DANGER

GASOLINE

use gasoline to start a barbecue or to clean tools. It's very dangerous, because gasoline can catch fire very easily. It produces invisible vapor, kind of like perfume does — you can smell it, but you can't see it.

Gasoline vapors are heavier than air, so they fall to the floor, creeping along silently and invisibly. They can burst into flames if they touch something hot (like a hot water heater) or get near a spark (like from a furnace). Gasoline fires happen and spread very quickly. That's why you should get away from the fire area as quickly as possible. The Fire Department should be called immediately. **Water should not be used to try and put out a gasoline fire.**

Because it's so dangerous, **gasoline should never be kept in the house**. If an adult uses gasoline in a lawn mower or engine, he or she should store only small amounts — in an approved safety container. It should be kept somewhere like a garage or shed that gets lots of fresh air. Adults must **never smoke when handling gasoline**. That includes at gas pumps, refueling the lawn mower, or carrying the gasoline can.

> **FIRE SAFETY TIP**
> Gasoline should NEVER be stored in the house.

NATURAL GAS & PROPANE

Lots of people heat their homes and run appliances (such as the stove) using natural gas and propane. These fuels are brought into homes through pipes and directed where they need to go.

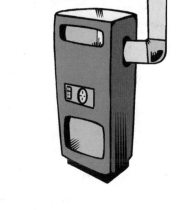

Children should NEVER turn on or light gas-burning appliances. For maximum safety, the burners and surfaces of the appliances should be kept clean and well maintained. Adults should regularly check the gas lines in the house for leaks and corrosion. The gas company should be contacted before anyone does any major digging in the soil at your place (since gas pipelines are buried).

Although natural gas has no scent, it is odorized so that you can smell it if there is a leak in the pipes. **A natural gas leak will smell like rotten eggs or a skunk.** If you ever smell what you believe to be a gas leak, tell an adult immediately.

These are important safety tips to know regarding gas or propane:

- Don't turn electrical switches on or off
- Open doors and windows to let gas escape
- Don't light matches or smoke
- If the odor is strong, everyone should get out of the house immediately, and then call the gas company

CARBON MONOXIDE

When natural gas burns efficiently, it mixes with the air to produce water vapor and carbon dioxide, which is harmless. But it will give off **carbon monoxide** (a deadly gas), if the conditions aren't right. This can happen when the appliance is not getting enough oxygen, for a variety of reasons, such as improper installation, blocked/cracked pipes, or materials blocking the base.

Carbon monoxide has no smell, so you won't know if it's in the air. But it will make you feel weak, nauseous, dizzy, and tired. It will also give you a headache, and if you're exposed to it long enough, it it can cause brain damage or even death.

To prevent carbon monoxide poisoning, gas appliances should be regularly checked and maintained. A **carbon monoxide detector should be installed in your home**.

If the alarm sounds, an adult should check the pilot lights on all appliances. If the alarm continues, the appliances should be shut off. Everyone should leave the house right away, and the gas company should be called from a neighbor's.

symbols to avoid

Some items may not only "burn", but can poison us, too. These are often things that your parents may use for cleaning the house, lighting the barbecue, getting rid of bugs, gardening, maintaining the car, and doing the laundry. As a result, many of these items may be somewhere in your house or garage. If you find one, you should **absolutely NEVER touch, shake, or taste it**. In fact, if one is within reach, ask your parent or an adult to put the item somewhere safe.

But how will you know if the items you've found are dangerous? You'll know because they'll be marked with symbols, or pictures that warn us. These symbols appear on the bottles, boxes, and cans of dangerous items.

> **FIRE SAFETY TIP**
>
> Always keep chemicals away from heat and fire.

If you see an item with any of the symbols that appear on the next page, don't touch it! **Never EVER shake, eat, or drink anything marked with one of these warnings**. These items are dangerous for kids to play with or use. They can burn, poison and kill!

Stay AWAY from these symbols!

CORROSIVE

EXPLOSIVE

POISONOUS

FLAMMABLE

no smoking, please!

S mart kids don't smoke, right? Of course not. It's unhealthy, expensive, and smells bad, too. But many older people (teenagers, parents, grandparents, and teachers) do smoke.

If your parents (or any other adults you know) smoke, here are some rules that will make your home, their home, and anywhere they smoke as safe as possible:

NO SMOKING PERMITTED

- NEVER smoke in bed!
- Use ashtrays that let the ashes and butts go down into a closed container.
- Don't empty ashtrays into the garbage bag or waste basket; instead, flush the ashes down the toilet.
- Don't leave matches, lighters, lighter fluid, or tobacco products (pipes, cigarettes, cigars) anywhere a kid can reach them.

review the rules

What have we learned so far? We understand that there are good and bad things about fire and heat.

Fire and heat are very useful and make our lives easier. We'll be safe, so long as everyone follows the rules of fire safety. Not only is it very important for us to know and

follow the rules — it's also very important to encourage everyone around us to know and follow them.

There are lots of rules and many places where we must follow them…at home, at school, in the playground, at camp — everywhere!

FIRE SAFETY RULES
- Never play with matches or lighters
- Never play with or near fireplaces, barbecues, camp fires, pilot lights
- Never play in the kitchen
- Never play with firecrackers

- Never play with or touch things marked **flammable**, **poison**, **explosive**, or **corrosive**
- Never play with electric cords
- Never play with Christmas tree lights
- Never play with or touch gasoline
- Never play with or touch a pilot light
- Never play with registers, radiators, or space heaters
- Never put a candle inside a jack-o-lantern
- Never empty ashtrays into the garbage bag or wastebaskets; flush the ashes down the toilet, instead
- Never go into a burning building or house

FIRE SAFETY TIP
Don't put anything metal in the microwave oven. It could start a fire.

- Always have an adult light birthday candles
- There should be a smoke alarm on every floor of your house
- Always have an adult check the smoke alarm batteries
- Draw a fire escape plan for your house, and make sure everyone knows the plan
- If you smell smoke in your house, alert your parents and follow your escape plan
- If your clothes catch fire: **stop**, **drop**, cover your face, and **roll**

- If you smell smoke away from home, someone should call the fire department or 911 (if you're old enough, you can do it yourself, see page 60)
- Never stick anything into the little holes of an electrical socket; you could get an electric shock

PLAY IT SAFE

Remember, these items are not toys. They can burn, poison, or kill. But **you won't be hurt if you don't touch or play with them**. So play it smart — and safe!

thought

- What would you do if you saw your best friend playing with a lighter?

- Why do you think kids shouldn't play in the kitchen?

- How would you feel if you caused a fire in your house by not playing safe?

- What can you do to keep your family safe from fire?

starters

part three

being prepared

smoke alarms

A **smoke alarm** is a small, dome-shaped device that can "smell" smoke. It's attached to the ceiling, and makes a loud, squealing noise when it detects something, alerting you to a possible fire. Smoke alarms are extremely important, because they can notify you of danger while you're asleep — or before you might have noticed on your own. Since smoke alarms save so many lives, they're required in all homes and buildings.

ONE ON EVERY FLOOR

Your home should have several smoke alarms to keep your family safe. If there are none, parents need to know that it's very important to get smoke alarms right away. In fact, there should be at least one on every floor of your house. A good rule to remember is that **there should be one smoke alarm for every person in the house, plus one more**. Smoke alarms should be placed outside every bedroom (in the hallway) or even in bedrooms.

TEST REGULARLY

Smoke alarms should be checked often, to ensure they are working. Have a parent **check the battery and test the alarm at least once a month**.

If you hear the smoke alarm (even if you don't smell smoke or see a fire), follow the instructions covered in the section "If you see a fire in your home" on page 55.

FIRE SAFETY TIP

Have your parents test the smoke alarm in front of you, so you'll know what it sounds like in case there really is a fire.

escape plans

An **escape plan** is a map of your house that shows how to get out when there's smoke or fire. It's important to have one and know it well so that you and your family can escape in case of an emergency.

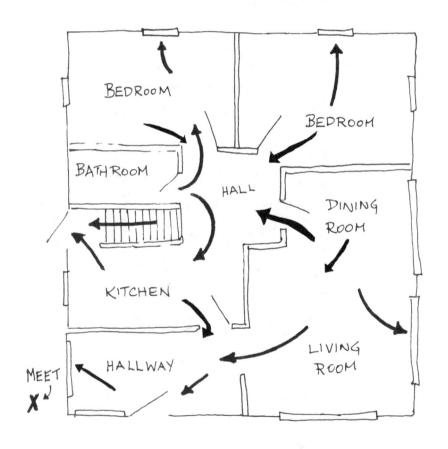

Your parents, babysitter and any other visitors should know the escape plan. They should practice it with you, so you'll know how to use it. If your family doesn't already have an escape plan, let them know how important it is to make one right away! It's a good idea to post the plan on the fridge or somewhere that it's easily visible to everyone in the house.

FIRE SAFETY TIP

Everybody in your house should know the family's escape plan very well.

DRAW YOUR OWN ESCAPE PLAN

On page 49 is a blank fire escape plan for you to fill in (or you can make one from scratch, using a plain sheet of paper). Create a floor plan of your house. In your plan, make sure to include all the doors, windows, stairs, walls, and anything that might get in the way of an escape. Each room should have (at least) two possible ways out. One should be a main route and the other a backup. For example, a main escape route from your bedroom might be through the door, while the backup escape route might be the window. Be sure to include all possible options in your plan.

SECOND FLOOR ESCAPE

Do you live in a two-story home? If so, there may be a need to escape through second floor windows. Parents need to plan for this possibility. Consider a non-combustible escape ladder if there's no way to climb out onto a balcony or roof.

MEETING PLACE

Your escape plan should also include a safe meeting place for everyone in your family to gather after they get out. It should be in front of your house, but far enough away that it's safe from the fire.

After you finish your plan, try it out with your family. Remember to revise your drawing if something in your house changes. Make sure that all main escape routes are kept clear and easy to use.

Practice the plan regularly so that everyone remembers what to do.

my escape plan

This is the escape plan we would use if we had to leave our home in a hurry. I'll practice it often so that I'll be able to remember it.

fire drills

A fire drill is similar to practicing a home escape plan, except that it takes place somewhere other than your home. **A fire drill teaches you what to do and where to go if a fire starts.** Most fire drills in which you'll participate will be at school.

Fire drills should be held often, so that you (and everyone else in your school) will know what to do in case of fire. Your teacher (or the person in charge) will tell you what to do during a fire drill. He or she will let you know the right way to leave your classroom and get outside.

Always listen to the person in charge, and follow the rules! That includes being quiet (so you can hear directions), walking — not running — during the drill, and proceeding single file.

FIRE ESCAPES

A fire escape is another way to leave a building and get outside. It may be a special stairway, a ladder attached to the exterior of a building, or some other means of escape. Your teacher or someone in charge will show you how to use it safely.

FIRE SAFETY TIP

After making your escape, do not return to the house or building until the fire department says it's safe to do so.

thought

- **Why do you think it's so important to have a smoke alarm on every floor?**

- **Why should everyone pay attention during a fire drill?**

- **Can you think of any ideas that will help remind your family members to test your smoke alarms?**

- **What are the benefits of an escape plan?**

starters

part four

responding to emergencies

four

when you hear the siren

You probably know what a siren sounds like. You also know that sirens are used by fire engines, ambulances, and other vehicles that are in a hurry. Usually, someone is hurt or could be hurt, so they're rushing to help.

If you hear a siren when you are outdoors playing, move away from the street. Stay well away until all the sirens have stopped. Even if you only see one emergency vehicle, there could be more coming past right away. **If you have a bicycle or toy with you, keep it clear of the street, too**. But if you've forgotten it there, DO NOT head out to get it until the sirens have stopped and it's safe to do so. Remember, the fire engine or emergency vehicles could be returning the same way, so you should be ready to stay out of the way.

If you're in a car and hear a siren, tell the car driver. He or she should pull over to the side of the road to let the fire engine (or emergency vehicle) pass.

if you see a fire in your home

I f you follow the rules of fire safety from section one, your chances of having an unwanted fire are much less. But if a fire does start — or if you smell or see smoke — here are some important rules to follow:

If you're the first person to hear the smoke alarm or smell smoke, **let an adult know IMMEDIATELY**. He or she will get you out of the house safely. When you get outside, wait at the designated meeting place. Don't go back into the house until the fire department tells you it's safe to return.

If you have learned your household's escape plan, this is the time to use it. Your parents or other adults will help you.

Leave the house right away and do NOT go back in to get clothing, toys, or pets.

Fire Safety RULE

If you live in an apartment or high-rise building, **do NOT use the elevator**. Escape via the fire exit (staircase) designated for such use.

Fire Safety RULE

If you or your parents, babysitter, or visitors have to call the Fire Department, this should be done after you have left the house. *Important:* **Get out first, THEN call the fire department** from a nearby house or building.

Fire Safety RULE

If your clothes catch fire, don't walk or run. **1) Stop**, **2) Drop** to the floor (covering your face), and **3) Roll** over and over until the fire has been put out. Do not try to put out the fire by beating it with your hands and don't pour water on it.

STOP　　　　**DROP**　　　　**ROLL**

Before opening any door along your escape route, kneel down and reach up to **touch the door with the back of your hand**. If it's not hot, touch the door handle with the back of your hand. If it feels warm or hot, use a different escape route. If the handle feels cool, open the door very cautiously and proceed, if safe.

If you run into smoke while you're escaping, try to use a different way out. If there's no other option, **crawl on your hands and knees to the exit, keeping your head low**.

If you're trapped in your bedroom, you can climb out the window if the room is on the first floor.

If you're trapped on the second floor or higher, don't go out the window unless there is an escape ladder or a balcony to climb out onto.

Fire Safety RULE

Stuff clothes or towels in the cracks under the door to keep smoke from coming in. Open the window a few inches, if possible, unless it seems to be drawing smoke into the room. If there's a working phone in the room, call the fire department and let them know where you are. They'll let the firefighters on the scene know where to find you. Stay by the window and wave a flashlight or light colored towel or sheet to help the firefighters see you.

Fire Safety RULE

Never hide from a firefighter! He or she is there to save you. Help the firefighter find you by calling out and waving your arms.

if you see a fire away from home

I f you're playing outside or walking to school and you smell or see smoke/fire coming from a house, school, store, or other building, there are things you can do to help.

- If there are adults close by, shout to them and let them know you have seen or smelled smoke or fire and where it is. Ask them to call the fire department.
- If no adults are nearby, run to a house, store, or building and let a grown-up know what you have seen or smelled. Ask him/her to call the fire department.
- If no one is nearby when you see or smell smoke or fire, and if you know where to find a telephone quickly — and if you are old enough to do it yourself — call 911 or the fire department and let them know where to go (see the page 60 for instructions).

FIRE SAFETY TIP
Never go into a house or any other building where you see or smell smoke or fire.

59

calling 9-1-1

These three numbers are very special and important. It's a phone number to be called in case of emergency, such as a fire. If there's no 911 emergency service in your area, dial the number of the fire department (you'll find it at the front of your phone book) and follow the steps described below:

1) Listen in the phone for the dial tone sound.
2) Dial 911 (or the emergency number for fire in your area).
3) When the emergency operator answers, say "I want to report a fire."
4) Give the address of the fire.
5) Listen **carefully**. You'll be asked questions (such as your name and the phone number from which you're calling).
6) Don't hang up until the operator says it's okay to.
7) Stay by the phone (if you're in a safe place) in case they call back.

If you're calling from a pay phone: listen for the dial tone and dial 911 or the fire department. If you don't get a dial tone, it means you need to put money in the phone.

pet safety during a fire

When making your escape, do not stop to look for a pet. The most important thing to remember is that you should get out safely and stay out. And you must **never, ever run back into a burning building to save a pet**.

Once the fire is over, take your pet to the veterinarian as soon as possible. The animal should be checked out for smoke inhalation and/or burns.

> **FIRE SAFETY TIP**
> Never go back into a burning building, no matter what.

thought

- Why do you think firefighters teach young people about fire safety?

- What would you do if you smelled smoke while walking home?

- Why must you leave a house fire without taking belongings?

- Would your family know what to do if a fire broke out in your home?

starters

part five

outdoor fire safety

forest fires

Did you know that millions of trees are burned every year by forest fires (also called wildfires)? Some forest fires start when trees are struck by lightning, but mostly, they're started by PEOPLE!

When there is a forest fire, many birds and animals are burned to death or have to leave their homes. People who enjoy going to the forest to camp or visit their cottages can no longer do so. After trees are lost to a fire, it takes many years for new ones to grow in their place. This is a problem because we need trees for many things in everyday life — such as furniture, newspapers, houses, boxes, and crates.

For all of these reasons, it's **VERY IMPORTANT** to know and follow the rules of fire safety when we are in the woods or forest.

campfires

Everyone loves a campfire. But they should only be made in campground or picnic areas where they're allowed. Campfires should ALWAYS be started, looked after, and put out by an adult.

Fires should not be made near trees — a spark could fly over and set the tree ablaze. As well, your campfire should not be near a tent, car, or anything that could easily ignite. Campfires should be

made below ground level (in a pit); rocks or stones should be placed all the way around the pit.

FIRE SAFETY TIP

If you or your clothes catch fire, don't panic. Stop, drop, cover your face, and roll.

KEEP YOUR DISTANCE
Everyone (especially kids) should stay a safe distance from the fire. Only the adult responsible for making the campfire should be close to it. After the fire has been

used for cooking — or is no longer needed — an adult should pour lots of water over the fire, stir the water into the ashes, then cover them with earth or sand.

FIRE SAFETY TIP

Only an adult should make or put out a campfire.

other outdoor fire safety rules

 Candles, matches, and fires should NEVER be used inside your tent.

 An adult should be in charge of any heaters, lanterns, and camp stoves that are used when camping.

 Smoking in the woods or in a campground can be very dangerous. If a cigarette or cigar butt (this is the part left when most of it has been smoked) is tossed away, it could easily continue to burn and cause a fire.

 No one should smoke inside a tent or camper.

 All cigarettes and cigars must be properly put out before leaving them. The best way to do this is by pouring water on them and covering them with earth or sand. (This is the same way we put out the campfire).

thought

- **What would you say if a friend suggested you build a bonfire?**

- **What would you do if you saw an adult toss a cigarette butt in the woods?**

- **How would you feel if someone you know caused a forest fire?**

- **Why do you think that most forest fires are actually caused by people?**

starters

part

**fire safety
for caregivers**

six

encourage learning

C hildren who read this book will learn a lot about fire safety. They should be encouraged to read and re-read the book until they can remember all the information inside.

Of course, active parental involvement is important, too. Encourage your kids by reviewing the book with them and practicing fire safety together. This interactivity will not only stimulate  successful learning for the kids, it will help keep fire safety fresh in the minds of everybody.

Although the fire safety concepts presented in this book have been simplified to make them easier for children to grasp, the rules of fire safety (and safety, in general) are very important for everyone, both young and old. Applying these common sense rules in your home and daily life will help you keep your family and property safe.

rules for parents

All parents and caregivers should know the basic rules for safety in the home. Some of the most well known ones are:

- Don't leave matches or lighters within the reach of children or in any place where kids are likely to find them (drawers, purses, pockets).

- Don't store flammable or poisonous materials or liquids anywhere children can obtain them.

- Don't leave children unattended in the presence of fire (fireplaces, stoves, barbecues, campfires, candles, bonfires, fireworks displays, etc.).

- Have an escape plan ready to use if fire breaks out in your home. (There should be two possible exits from each room). Rehearse it with your kids regularly, so that they are very familiar with it.

- Space heaters should be used with care and kept away from combustibles.

- Use large address numbers on your house, to help the fire department identify it easily.

- Never smoke in bed!

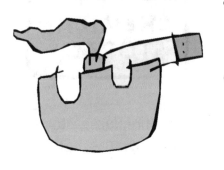

- Never smoke while under the effects of medication!

- Never smoke while drowsy — including while under the influence of alcohol!

- Never empty ashtrays into garbage containers or wastebaskets. They should be emptied into a non-combustible container with a lid or a container outside.

- Have smoke/heat alarms installed on each level of your home and outside of sleeping areas. The alarms should be tested monthly to make sure they're always working.

- Keep a fire extinguisher easily accessible in the home; an appropriate model is a 2A 10BC type. These can be used on ordinary combustibles, flammable liquids, and electrical fires.

- Don't remain in your home if fire breaks out. Make sure everyone leaves, then go to the nearest telephone to call the fire department. Do not return to the home until and unless the fire department allows you to.

- Don't allow children to use or play with Christmas tree lights, candles, electrical cords, or jack-o-lanterns.

- Ensure your kids' Halloween costumes are made out of non-flammable materials. Rather than masks or other face and head coverings, use makeup to "paint" their disguises.

- Don't allow children to play in the kitchen, whether you're present or not; even if cooking isn't being done.

- Don't allow pot handles to extend beyond the stovetop; point them away from the front of the stove, but be sure they are not above another hot burner. Burns and scalds from heated food, water or grease can be disfiguring and even fatal!

- Don't allow children to prepare their own bath water. Always test the water temperature before the child enters the bath and stay during bath time.

- If you're having guests, be sure everyone knows your escape plan. If anyone is disabled, make a point of ensuring there is a safe fire escape route that accounts for the disability.

- Ensure that appropriate first aid information is readily available, in case someone suffers a burn or other injury during a fire.

- Keep electrical appliances away from water or wet areas.

- A fireplace should have a proper screen or cover to keep sparks and wood in (and children and pets out).

- In case of fire, before trying to exit through a door, test the door, then the doorknob with the back of your hand to see if it's hot. If it is, use a different escape route. If the handle feels cool, open the door very cautiously and proceed.

- Keep a copy of the escape plan handy for babysitters and anyone staying in the home.

- Never put anything metal in the microwave oven; it could start a fire.

- Prevent burns by wearing gloves and other protective clothing when you handle chemicals.

- Put covers on any electrical outlets that are within children's reach.

- Set the temperature on your hot water heater to 120 degrees Fahrenheit (49 degrees celsius) or use the "low-medium" setting. Water hotter than this can cause burns within two or three seconds.

- Use cool-water vaporizers. Hot steam vaporizers can cause burns if you get too close to them.

- Never wear clothing with long, loose sleeves while you're cooking.

- Before putting a child into a car seat, touch the seat to see how hot it is. Hot seat belt straps and buckles can cause second-degree burns on small children. Cover the car seat with a towel if you park in the sun.

- Don't overload electrical receptacles.

- Don't use light bulbs with wattage greater than a fixture can handle.

- Leave plenty of air space around appliances and television sets; they can overheat and catch fire.

- Don't let combustible materials such as newspapers and rags pile up in basements or garages.

- Don't let soot (creosote) build up in the chimney, fireplace, or heating stove.

- Don't let lint build up in the clothes dryer.

- Place candles on a flat, stable surface, away from curtains and furniture — and out of reach of children and pets.

- Use proper candleholders and always place them on heat-resistant surfaces, like a ceramic plate (never on polished surfaces, like televisions).

- Never try to move a candle once it's lit.

fire safety rules for teachers

- See to it that fire drills are performed regularly.

- Consider having a fire drill when a new term starts or a new child joins the class.

- If your school has fire escapes, be sure the children know where they are and are comfortable with using them.

- Remind the kids that they must stay calm during a fire drill, pay attention, walk (not run), and proceed single file.

fire safety rules for babysitters

- Be sure to familiarize yourself with the family's fire escape plan.

- Don't let the kids play with or use any of the dangerous items mentioned in this book.

- If fire breaks out, get the children out of the house immediately, then go for help, then notify the parents (in that order).

- Be sure you know where to reach the parents in case of emergency.

more information

I t's very important for everyone to know as much as possible about fire safety (and all types of safety, for that matter). Although we can only cover so much in this book, there's a lot of detailed information out there. We recommend that all readers — children, parents, teachers, babysitters, grandparents, and other family members — gather as much information as they can about fire safety.

Start by calling or visiting your local fire department or checking out books at your nearest library. Government offices and fire prevention equipment suppliers may also be of help. Of course, the Internet is a wealth of information on all kinds of topics, including fire safety.

Here are some web sites (including some kid-friendly ones) to help you begin your search:
- **www.usfa.fema.gov/kids/**
- **www.nfpa.org**
- **www.smokeybear.com**
- **www.survivealive.org/main**
- **www.gov.on.ca/OFM/**

part

first aid tips

seven

HYPOTHERMIA

Shivering, slurred speech, stumbling and drowsiness after cold exposure are indications of hypothermia. Condition is severe when shivering stops. Unconsciousness and stopped breathing may follow.

- Transfer gently to shelter. Movement or rough handling can upset heart rhythm.
- Remove wet clothing; wrap in warm covers.
- Re-warm neck, chest, abdomen and groin — but not extremities; apply direct body heat or safe heating devices.
- Give warm drinks, if conscious.
- Monitor breathing; give artificial respiration if needed.
- Call for medical aid or transport gently.

BURNS AND SCALDS

The size, location, and depth determine how serious a burn is and whether the person's life is in danger. Burns on infants and the elderly are always serious.

- Immerse the burn area in cool water; this will relieve pain and slow or stop the burning process.
- Cover the burn with dry, sterile dressing (don't use ointments); bandage lightly.
- Monitor breathing when the burns are around the face.
- Transport to medical aid.

UNCONSCIOUSNESS

Loss of consciousness may threaten life if the person is on his/her back and the tongue has dropped to the back of the throat, blocking the airway.

- Ensure that the person is

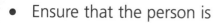

breathing before seeking the cause of unconsciousness.
- If injuries permit, place the casualty in the recover position with the neck extended.
- Never give anything to an unconscious casualty by mouth.

FRACTURES
- Steady and support the injury. Do not move the victim.
- Dress wounds and control the bleeding.
- If the injured person must be moved, secure the limb with bandages over padded splints.
- Check for signs of a pulse beyond the fracture or joint injury. (If no pulse, get medical aid quickly!)
- Hold neck and back injuries steady and call for help.
- Reassure the injured person and keep him/her warm to prevent shock.

HEAT EXHAUSTION

Heat exhaustion is a shock-like condition caused by exposure — especially in the elderly and persons in poor physical condition.

- Move the person out of the heat; place at rest.
- Loosen tight clothing.
- Keep the person's head low; raise his/her feet and legs slightly
- For cramps, give a glass of slightly salted, cool water to drink (add ¼ teaspoon of salt). Repeat no more than once.
- Watch breathing.
- Get medical aid.

FROSTBITE

Frostbite makes the skin white, waxy, and numb; freezing causes hardening.

- Warm the frostbitten area gradually with body heat; do not rub.

- Do not thaw frozen hands and feet unless medical aid is far away and there is no chance of re-freezing; they are better thawed in hospital.
- If there are blisters, apply sterile dressings and bandage lightly to prevent breaking.
- Get to medical aid.

EYE INJURIES

- Do not attempt to remove particles on the pupil or stuck to the eyeball. Other loose particles should be removed with care.

- Remove loose particles with a moistened corner of a tissue.
- If this fails, cover the eye lightly with a dressing, cover the other eye to prevent movement and transport to medical aid.

MEDICATIONS

Treat medications with the respect they deserve, showing proper regard for safety and effectiveness. There are five "rights" to be observed:

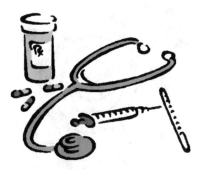

- right medication
- right person
- right amount
- right time
- right method

NOSE BLEEDS

- Sit down with the head slightly forward.
- Loosen clothing around the neck and breathe through the mouth.
- Pinch the nose just below the cartilage for about 10 minutes.
- Do not sniff or blow nose for several hours.
- Cold compresses may be applied to the forehead and the nape of the neck.
- Use a wet hankie or cloth to clean the area around the nose.

- If bleeding persists or recurs, it may be a sign of some medical problem; seek medical attention.

EMBEDDED OBJECT

Do not attempt to pull out objects embedded in a wound. Pulling at nails, splinters, or a piece of glass in a wound will only cause more damage and increase bleeding.

- Dress the wound lightly without putting pressure on the object.
- Secure the padding with bandages so as to apply pressure around the wound and away from the object.
- Get medical aid.

SNAKE BITE

- Calm and reassure the bite victim; fear increases the degree of shock.
- Lay the person down; movement stimulates circulation and speeds the spread of poison through the body.
- Flush the wound with soapy water and wash away all venom around the wound.
- Support the limb and keep it still.

- Obtain immediate medical aid.
- Kill the snake, for identification (if possible).
- Start artificial respiration, if necessary.
- If you think the snake is poisonous, apply a flat constrictive bandage above the bite — that is,

between it and the heart; the bandage should be loose enough to insert a finger and should not stop circulation below it; it may be loosened hourly and removed in three hours if no symptoms develop.
- Keep the limb lowered, supported, and immobilized if necessary.
- Do not cool or use ice packs.

WOUNDS AND BLEEDING
- Use direct pressure to stop blood flow.
- Elevate to reduce blood flow.
- Rest to slow the circulation.
- Apply direct pressure with the hand over a dressing if available; if the dressing becomes blood soaked, do not remove it; add another and continue pressure.
- When bleeding is controlled, maintain pressure and

secure dressings with bandages.
- Maintain elevation and immobilize the injured limb.

ARTIFICIAL RESPIRATION

Someone who has stopped breathing may suffer brain damage after four minutes and die within ten minutes. Mouth-to-mouth resuscitation puts air into the lungs until the victim can breathe again.

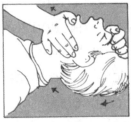

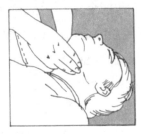

- Check for breathing — look, listen, and feel for air movement.
- If not breathing, open the airway — with one hand on the forehead and the fingers of the other hand on the bony part of the jaw, tilt the head backward.
- If breathing does not start, begin artificial respiration immediately.
- Pinch the nose closed with

your fingers and blow two full breaths into the victim's mouth, pausing in between to take a deep breath yourself.

- Look, listen, and feel for air exchange. Check the neck pulse. If there is a pulse but no breathing, continue giving one breath every five seconds.
- **For infants:** cover both nose and mouth and breathe gently; one breath every three seconds for both child and infant.

CONSCIOUS CHOKING CASUALTY

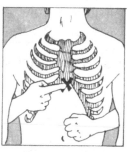

- Do not interfere with a person who is choking, as long as he/she can speak, breathe, and cough forcefully.
- When he/she can no longer do these things, have someone call for an ambulance and begin the Heimlich maneuver:
- Stand behind the person and, with your arms around him/her, clench your fist and thrust it, thumb knuckle inward, at a spot well below

the breastbone, slightly above the navel, and well
away from either side of the rib cage.

- Hold your fist with the other hand and pull both hands
toward you with a quick upward-and-inward thrust
from the elbows.
- Repeat continuously until the blockage is dislodged or
the victim becomes unconscious.

UNCONSCIOUS CHOKING CASUALTY
This situation may require CPR. If someone nearby is
trained in this procedure, have him or her administer
immediately. Either way, call for emergency medical service.

part
fun, learning
& graduation
eight

fill in the blanks

1) _____ alarms save lives.

2) Plan an _____ route and practice it often.

3) Never put a _____
inside a jack-o-lantern.

4) _____ go back into
a burning building.

5) _____ means to
burn yourself with water.

6) If your clothes catch on fire, you should _____, drop,
cover your _____ and _____ on the ground.

7) The emergency phone number is _____.

8) Never _____ with matches.

9) Kids should not play in the _____.

10) It's important to follow the rules of _____ safety.

94

fire safety quiz

et's see how much you remember. Here are some questions about fire safety. If you know the answer, write it down under the question. If you don't remember it, you'll be able to find the answer in the book by turning to the page listed. Afterward, go back and read the book again. This will help you remember the important rules of fire safety!

1) List three "good" uses for fire (page 15): _____,

_____, and _____.

2) Why is the kitchen a dangerous place to play? (Page 22)

_____

_____

_____

3) What is a "flashover"? (Page 23)

_____

_____

4) How long does it take for a simple flame to get out of control? (Page 23) _____

5) Why is it unsafe for kids to touch a barbecue? (Page 25)
_____

6) What is a "pilot light"? (Page 26)
_____

7) Why should you never touch a pilot light? (Page 26)
_____

8) What can happen if you play with Christmas tree lights or the electric power cord? (Page 27)
_____

9) What light source should be used for the inside of a jack-o-lantern? (Page 28) _____

10) What's dangerous about being in the sun? (Page 31)
_____

11) True or false? Water should be used to put out a gasoline fire. (Page 32) _____

12) What does a natural gas leak smell like? (Page 33)

_____

13) How would you know if there's carbon monoxide in the air? (Page 34)

_____

_____

14) Name the four hazardous warning symbols that let us know an item is dangerous to handle. (Pages 37)

_____, _____

_____, _____

15) How should ashtrays be emptied? (Page 38)

_____

16) Why are smoke alarms so important? (Page 44)

_____

17) What's the rule regarding how many smoke alarms should be in a house? (Page 44)

_____

_____

18) What's an escape plan? (Page 46)

_____

19) In an escape plan, each room should have how many ways out? (Page 47) _____

20) Where should your family's meeting place be? (Page 48)

_____

21) What are fire drills for? (Page 50)

_____

22) How were fires fought before fire engines were invented? (Page 18)

_____

23) What do firefighters do when they're not busy fighting fires? (Pages 19-20)

_____

_____

_____

24) What should you do when you hear a siren while you're outside playing? In a car? (Page 54)

_____

_____

_____

_____

25) What should you do if your clothes catch fire? (Page 56)

_____, _____

_____ & _____

26) What should you do before opening any doors along your escape route? (Page 57)

_____

_____

27) If you're trapped in a burning building, how should you let the firefighters know where to find you? (Page 58)

_____

_____

28) What's the main rule regarding pets in a fire ? (Page 61)

_____

_____

29) Where should campfires be made? (Page 65)

_____

30) How should a campfire be put out? By whom? (Page 66)

_____

_____

_____

coloring time!

Stay low in smoke!

In case of smoke, always crawl
low on your hands and knees.

USE THIS SPACE TO DRAW YOUR OWN
FIRE RESCUE SCENE

USE THIS SPACE TO DRAW YOUR OWN

FIRE PREVENTION POSTER

106

games & puzzles

WORD SEARCH

Can you find these hidden words? **(Solutions on Page 111)**

SMOKE	LADDER	CAMPFIRE
ALARM	HEATER	PROPANE
FIRE	FLAMMABLE	FURNACE
FIREFIGHTER	ASHTRAY	COOKING
ENGINE	COMBUSTIBLE	SCALD
GASOLINE	ESCAPE PLAN	WATER
SAFETY	DRILL	FIREPLACE

A	E	Y	D	E	J	W	A	I	R	K	L	O	E	F	U	E	D	N	V	K
I	K	G	J	U	T	U	X	Y	S	D	U	C	H	I	G	U	Y	W	E	Y
P	O	F	F	I	R	E	P	L	A	C	E	H	E	R	I	F	P	M	A	C
K	R	E	D	D	A	L	J	J	R	G	B	G	N	O	E	T	G	K	U	R	U
E	F	S	D	E	E	C	S	A	O	R	T	R	U	F	N	V	G	X	Z	J
U	U	T	E	Q	D	R	J	R	D	P	W	P	K	I	R	G	N	K	T	I
H	C	W	E	A	D	H	S	H	S	O	A	I	E	G	W	H	I	S	A	H
E	O	H	R	S	M	O	K	E	L	P	T	N	S	H	J	F	K	N	P	O
H	M	L	E	X	F	F	H	A	B	D	E	O	E	T	A	Y	O	X	E	K
P	B	W	U	E	R	B	V	T	M	C	R	P	E	E	R	N	O	L	E	N
F	U	R	N	A	C	E	G	E	A	E	L	L	I	R	D	S	C	P	M	A
F	S	E	M	F	A	O	M	R	A	L	A	G	E	U	C	B	D	F	O	L
M	T	C	G	H	R	R	E	B	O	G	H	E	A	H	S	V	L	H	N	P
O	I	X	E	P	W	N	L	U	O	Z	A	S	H	T	R	A	Y	O	T	E
N	B	U	E	S	I	H	X	P	E	I	H	D	E	A	M	V	N	B	H	P
B	L	Z	M	L	O	E	O	S	S	A	E	B	I	M	Z	N	N	R	P	A
F	E	V	O	I	R	M	P	C	C	N	E	D	A	W	E	F	M	I	O	C
L	N	S	W	R	U	O	T	F	S	A	M	B	V	R	A	E	I	T	T	S
S	A	F	E	T	Y	P	F	T	O	D	L	B	L	M	I	Y	Z	R	L	E
G	N	B	N	O	E	O	I	M	M	E	S	D	A	Q	R	H	O	U	E	D

DECODER

Use this code to uncover the fire safety messages below:

A=5 B=7 C=13 D=22 E=19 F=10 G=25 H=17
I=15 J=8 K=23 L=9 M=1 N=12 O=14 P=24
Q=2 R=11 S=4 T=18 U=26 V=21 W=3 X=16
Y=6 Z=20

___ ___ __ ___   __ _ __ __ __
18 19 4 18   4 1 14 23 19

__ _ __ __ _ __   __ __   __
5 9 5 11 1 4   14 12   5

__ __ __ __ _ __ __   _ __ __ __ __
11 19 25 26 9 5 11   7 5 4 15 4

__ __ _ __ __ __ __ __   __ __ __ __   __ __ __ __ __ __
24 11 5 13 18 15 13 19   6 14 26 11   19 4 13 5 24 19

__ __ _ __   __ __ __ __   __ __ __ __   __ __ __ __ __ __
24 9 5 12   3 15 18 17   6 14 26 11   10 5 1 15 9 6

— — — — —   — —   — — — —   — — — —   —
12 19 21 19 11   25 14   7 5 13 23   15 12 18 14   5

— — — — — — —   — — — — — — — —
7 26 11 12 15 12 25   7 26 15 9 22 15 12 25

— — — —   — — — — — —   — — —   — — — — —
23 15 22 4   4 17 14 26 9 22   12 14 18   18 14 26 13 17

— — — — — — —   — —   — — — — — — — —
1 5 18 13 17 19 4   14 11   9 15 25 17 18 19 11 4

— — — — — — — —   — — — — —   — —
19 21 19 11 6 14 12 19   12 19 19 22 4   18 14

— — — — — — —   — — —   — — — — —   — —
10 14 9 9 14 3   18 17 19   11 26 9 19 4   14 10

— — — —   — — — — — —
10 15 11 19   4 5 10 19 18 6

(Solutions on Page 111)

FIRE MAZE

Can you help the fire engine find its way through the maze to go put out the fire?

START HERE!

PUZZLE SOLUTIONS

WORD SEARCH

A	E	Y	D	E	J	W	A	I	R	K	L	O	E	F	U	E	D	N	V	K
I	K	G	J	U	T	U	X	Y	S	D	U	C	H	I	G	U	Y	W	E	Y
P	O	F	F	I	R	E	P	L	A	C	E	H	E	R	I	F	P	M	A	C
K	R	E	D	D	A	L	J	R	G	B	G	N	O	E	T	G	K	U	R	U
E	F	S	D	E	E	C	S	A	O	R	T	R	U	F	N	V	G	X	Z	J
U	U	T	E	Q	D	R	J	R	D	P	W	P	K	I	R	G	N	K	T	I
H	C	W	E	A	D	H	S	H	S	O	A	I	E	G	W	H	I	S	A	H
E	O	H	R	S	M	O	K	E	L	P	T	N	S	H	J	F	K	N	P	O
H	M	L	E	X	F	F	H	A	B	D	E	O	E	T	A	Y	O	X	E	K
P	B	W	U	E	R	B	V	T	M	C	R	P	E	E	R	N	O	L	E	N
F	U	R	N	A	C	E	G	E	A	E	L	L	I	R	D	S	C	P	M	A
F	S	E	M	F	A	O	M	R	A	L	A	G	E	U	C	B	D	F	O	L
M	T	C	G	H	R	R	E	B	O	G	H	E	A	H	S	V	L	H	N	P
O	I	X	E	P	W	N	L	U	O	Z	A	S	H	T	R	A	Y	O	T	E
N	B	U	E	S	I	H	X	P	E	I	H	D	E	A	M	V	N	B	H	P
B	L	Z	M	L	O	E	O	S	S	A	E	B	I	M	Z	N	N	R	P	A
F	E	V	O	I	R	M	P	C	C	N	E	D	A	W	E	F	M	I	O	C
L	N	S	W	R	U	O	T	F	S	A	M	B	V	R	A	E	I	T	T	S
S	A	F	E	T	Y	P	F	T	O	D	L	B	L	M	I	Y	Z	R	L	E
G	N	B	N	O	E	O	I	M	M	E	S	D	A	Q	R	H	O	U	E	D

DECODER MESSAGES:

1) TEST SMOKE ALARMS ON A REGULAR BASIS

2) PRACTICE YOUR ESCAPE PLAN WITH YOUR FAMILY

3) NEVER GO BACK INTO A BURNING BUILDING

4) KIDS SHOULD NOT TOUCH MATCHES OR LIGHTERS

5) EVERYONE NEEDS TO FOLLOW THE RULES OF FIRE SAFETY

autographs

These are the autographs of my friends at the fire department:

MY FIRE CHIEF:

MY FIREFIGHTERS:

important telephone numbers

MY HOME PHONE NUMBER: _____

MY DAD'S NUMBER AT WORK: _____

MY MOM'S NUMBER AT WORK: _____

MY SCHOOL'S NUMBER: _____

OUR FIRE DEPARTMENT'S NUMBER: _____

OUR POLICE DEPARTMENT'S NUMBER:_____

OUR DOCTOR'S NUMBER:
_____

OUR HOSPITAL'S NUMBER:

_____

POISON TREATMENT NUMBER:

_____

GAS COMPANY'S NUMBER:

_____

This is to certify that

_____

has successfully completed the Community Safety Net program

Fire Safety for Kids

COMMUNITY
Safety
Net

Date: _____   Instructor: _____

PROTECTING KIDS FOR LIFE

A pledge for my future

I respect myself and I want to protect my future. That's why I'm making the following commitment:

This pledge may be revised on my ____ birthday.

I, _____, solemnly promise to abide by the rules of fire safety, as I've learned in "Fire Safety for Kids".

Signature: _____   Date: _____

Fire Prevention Officer: _____

HEY KIDS! WANT TO WIN YOUR VERY OWN
COMPUTER?

Write us a letter! Each month, we'll draw names for t-shirts and at year end, we'll choose the best one and give the winner a BRAND NEW COMPUTER!

IN YOUR LETTER, TELL US:

▸ How the program has changed the way you think or feel about fire safety, and the potential fire hazards around your home
▸ How you plan to use what you've learned from the program to make yourself and others safe
▸ Why you think safety education is important for young people

WE WANT TO HEAR FROM YOUR PARENTS, TOO!

Parental involvement is an important part of a young person's learning process. Parents, please show your support by including a comment with your child's letter, expressing how you feel this safety program has impacted your kids.

SEND YOUR LETTERS TO: "Mr. Computer Contest"

385 DeBaets Street **Winnipeg, MB R2J 4J8** **CANADA**	OR	**276 Cavalier St., P.O. Box 559** **Pembina, ND 58271-0559** **UNITED STATES**

or e-mail us at mr.computer@communitysafetynet.com

COMMUNITY
Safety
Net